I want to be a SCIENTIST

I want to be a SCIENTIST

Written by **Štěpánka Sekaninová**
Illustrated by **Honza Smolík**

* CONTENTS *

* INTRODUCTION *

Anthropology, dendrology, bryology, paleontology, archaeology, biology, pedology… All these tricky-to-pronounce words end in "-ology." But what does that ending mean? It simply refers to a science or field of study. Scientists in these fields—anthropologists, dendrologists, bryologists, paleontologists, archaeologists, biologists, pedologists, and more—are called "-ologists."

Now for the big question: Do you know what a dendrologist, meteorologist, anthropologist, bryologist, or herpetologist does? Maybe not? No worries—you're about to find out! This book is packed with descriptions of scientists and their fascinating fields. You might already know what a teacher, actor, salesperson, or doctor does, but what about these specialists? By the time you finish reading, you might just discover a little scientist hiding inside. Let's get started!

* PALEONTOLOGIST *

A PALEONTOLOGIST IS FASCINATED BY FOSSILS AND OTHER REMAINS OF ANCIENT LIFE ON PLANET EARTH. LIKE AN ARCHAEOLOGIST (ANOTHER SCIENTIST WHO STUDIES THE PAST), THEY ARE EAGER TO UNCOVER SECRETS FROM DEEP IN THE SOIL, UNDERGROUND, OR EMBEDDED IN ROCK.

DIFFERENCES BETWEEN PALEONTOLOGISTS AND ARCHAEOLOGISTS

Whereas archeologists focus on objects and other traces left behind by ancient humans, paleontologists study the plants and animals that lived on Earth millions of years ago. Over time, the remains of these organisms have turned to stone, or fossilized. Paleontologists work to uncover these fossils.

WHAT FOSSILS REVEAL

Fossils show paleontologists what ancient organisms looked like, what they ate, what hunted them, and how the plants and animals of the past are connected to those of today.

HURRAY FOR ROCKS!

Fossils are scattered all over the world. Before we can see them in a museum, they must first be discovered and extracted from rock by paleontologists.

FOSSIL HUNTING

Not all rocks contain fossils. A paleontologist uses their knowledge and experience to find the right ones. This work goes beyond simple detective skills. Fossils are not found in igneous rocks—those formed from cooling lava or magma—nor in metamorphic rocks, which are created by heat and pressure transforming other rocks. Instead, fossils are found in sedimentary rocks. If a plant or animal becomes trapped in the settling sediment, it has a chance of becoming fossilized.

A PALEONTOLOGIST'S EQUIPMENT

CHISELS

WALKIE-TALKIE

SCREWDRIVER

ROCK HAMMER

BRUSHES

GPS LOCATOR

SLEDGEHAMMER

SPATULAS AND SCRAPERS

SPECIMEN CONTAINER

CIRCULAR SAW

JACKHAMMER

ONCE A FOSSIL IS FOUND

A paleontologist spends time working both indoors in a lab and outdoors "in the field" not necessarily an actual field, like a wheat field—this just means working outside in nature, where plants and animals live. After paleontologists find fossils, they study them to learn about ancient plants and animals. They try to figure out what these creatures were like, how they changed over time, and how the Earth itself has changed.

ROCK SPECIMENS

GAIZE

GABBRO

GRANITE

BASALT

COAL

LIMESTONE

IT'S NOT JUST ABOUT FOSSILS

Paleontologists don't just study fossilized shells or ancient sea creatures like trilobites. They also examine the fossilized bones of prehistoric animals—not only dinosaurs, but also the ancient ancestors of animals we know today. By studying these bones, paleontologists can learn what these creatures looked like, how they moved, what they ate, and how they lived.

Where does this bone go? Any ideas?

Trilobites, dinosaurs, prehistoric lizards—this is your world. You spot a promising rock and immediately start studying it. What if it contains a rare fossil? Could a career as a paleontologist be in your future?

TYPES OF PALEONTOLOGY

PALEOBOTANY – specializes in prehistoric plants.
PALEOZOOLOGY – specializes in prehistoric animals.
PALEOECOLOGY – examines relations between prehistoric organisms and their environments.
MICROPALEONTOLOGY – studies microfossils.

* ARCHAEOLOGIST *

AN ARCHAEOLOGIST LOVES TO DIG IN THE GROUND IN SEARCH OF OBJECTS AND REMAINS FROM LONG-AGO CIVILIZATIONS. FRAGMENTS OF POTS, COINS, RUINS, BURIAL SITES, PREHISTORIC WASTE—SUCH ARTIFACTS BRING JOY TO ARCHAEOLOGISTS! THESE DISCOVERIES HELP THEM UNDERSTAND HOW HUMANS LIVED IN THE DISTANT PAST. WHEN EXPLORING BURIAL SITES, ARCHAEOLOGISTS MUST SEEK PERMISSION FROM DESCENDANT COMMUNITIES AND TREAT ALL FINDINGS WITH GREAT CARE AND RESPECT.

WHAT IS AN ARTIFACT?

An artifact is something made or modified for a specific purpose. Artifacts can be classified as movable or immovable, by their material (bone, metal, ceramic, wood, etc.), or by the purpose for which they were created (e.g., vessel, weapon, jewelry, fortification, grave, toy).

If a mysterious tool dug from the earth excites you, if you dream of discovering the remnants of a medieval platter or the grave of a distant ancestor, and if you're passionate about history, then archaology may be the perfect career for you!

DETECTIVE ON A DIG

Nothing excites an archaeologist like the start of a dig. Will they uncover the remnants of a settlement or rare treasures? Along with handling a shovel, an archaeologist must be good with a pencil and graph paper to map out the location and details of their discoveries. Using a surveying tool, they measure the area and mark the exact spots where objects are found.

CLEANLINESS IS NEXT TO GODLINESS

An object that has been buried in the ground for centuries won't be clean. So, what should be done? An archaeologist must wash it carefully—very carefully—using only water and a toothbrush.

STICKING THINGS TOGETHER

Many archaeologists love jigsaw puzzles. If a skilled archaeologist finds many fragments—or sherds—of the same ceramic, they carefully piece them together. Fragments with decoration or with the same thickness are the easiest to put together. Next step? Figuring out how ancient people used the object.

A DRAWING IS A MUST

Once those hundreds of fragments have been put back together into a pot, the preserved find must be documented with a careful, accurate drawing on paper. At this stage, scientists who don't draw well often seek the help of professional illustrators.

LIKE SHERLOCK HOLMES

The terrain has been fully explored, and all artifacts have been dug up, documented, described, numbered, and drawn in detail. Still, one part of the archaeologist's work remains. As they examine the finds closely, they draw conclusions about our ancestors' lives, and then go on to write a report or article about them, or even, in time, a whole book.

AN ARCHAEOLOGIST'S EQUIPMENT

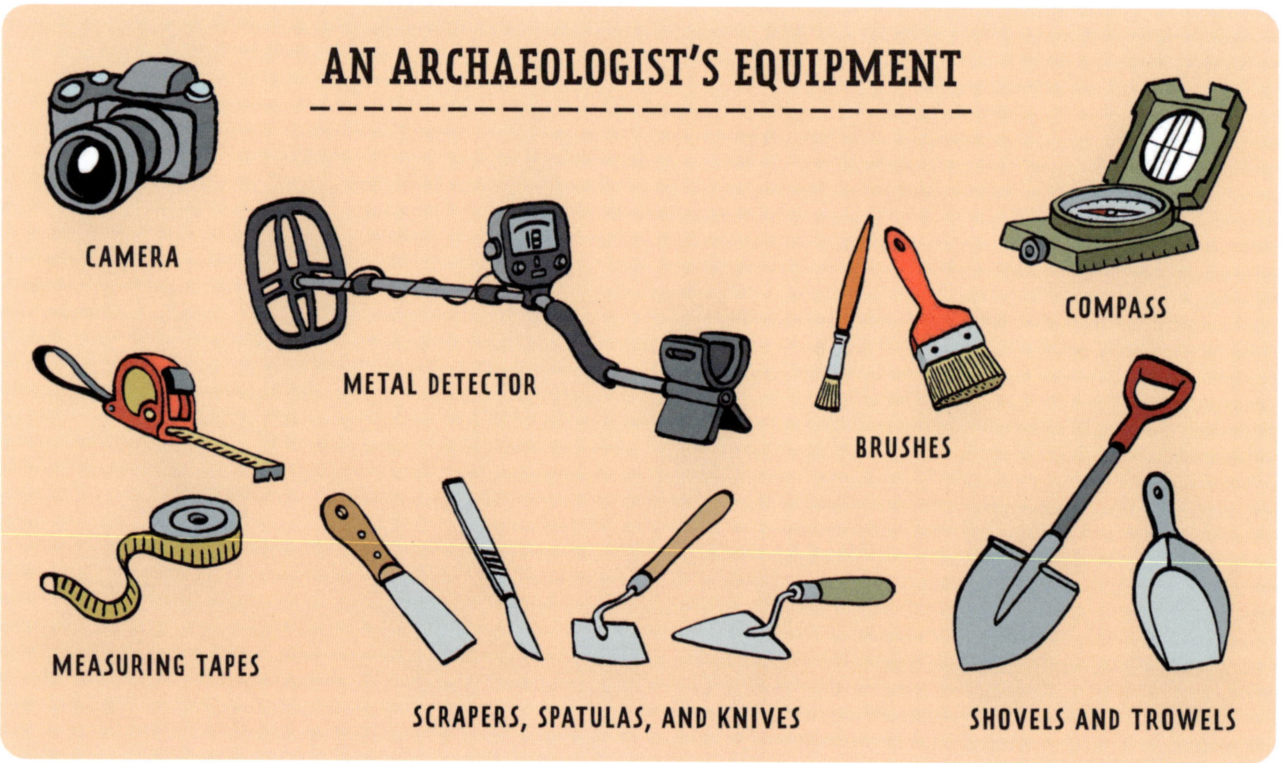

IMMOVABLE ARTIFACTS
REMAINS OF A MEDIEVAL SETTLEMENT
MOVABLE ARTIFACTS
CERAMIC REMNANTS: HORSE FIGURINE, MORTAR, POTS
BRONZE PIN
BRONZE SWORD
BRONZE CLASP
BRONZE SPEAR (POINT)

* BRYOLOGIST *

A BRYOLOGIST IS A SCIENTIST WHOSE PASSION IS MOSS AND OTHER BRYOPHYTES. THE MOMENT THEY SEE MOSS, THEY MUST IMMEDIATELY EXAMINE, OBSERVE, DESCRIBE, AND CLASSIFY IT. A BRYOLOGIST ALSO TRAVELS A LOT IN SEARCH OF MOSS. THE MORE SPECIES THEY DISCOVER, THE HAPPIER THEY ARE. INSTEAD OF TAKING A BREAK IN THE OPEN AIR, THEY LIE ON THEIR BELLY IN THE MIDDLE OF A FOREST, HARD AT WORK. IF YOU MEET THEM IN THE FIELD, YOU'LL SEE THEM STUDYING MOSS UP CLOSE.

WHAT A BRYOLOGIST DOES

A bryologist studies moss by collecting different types to examine closely. Their goal is to describe and understand all kinds of moss and other bryophytes—small plants that don't have flowers or roots. Bryologists treat moss with deep respect because it's one of the oldest land plants. Moss has been growing in nearly the same form since the Paleozoic era, making it a kind of living fossil.

Do you see a mossy glade as more than just a soft spot to rest and instead, start looking closely at tiny plants and lichens? You are on your way to becoming a bryologist!

THERE'S MOSS AND THERE'S MOSS

Don't think bryologists spend all their time in mossy forests. Moss shows up in surprising places—like around a dripping faucet or between windows on a bus.

WHY MOSS?

This humble plant is great at holding water, and helping to prevent floods. Moss is also one of the first plants to grow back after a fire, providing an important water source for other plants.

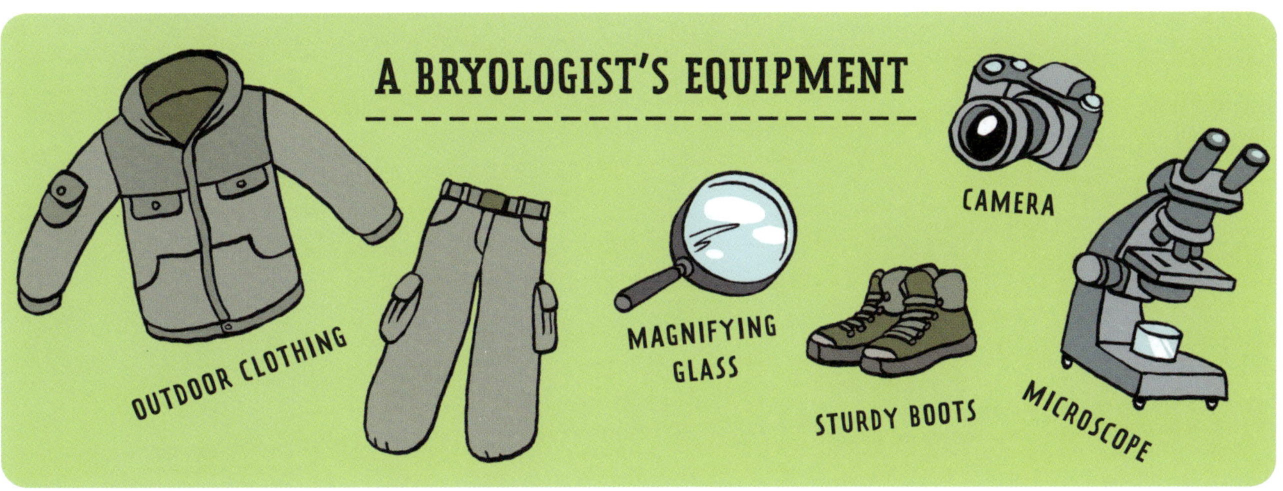

* ICHTHYOLOGIST *

AN ICHTHYOLOGIST LOVES WATER AND EVERYTHING THAT LIVES IN IT—FISH BIG AND SMALL, JAWLESS OR CARTILAGINOUS, EVEN SHARKS. THEY SPEND THEIR TIME OBSERVING, STUDYING, AND EXAMINING THESE CREATURES, SO THEY KNOW A TON ABOUT THEM. ICHTHYOLOGISTS STUDY HOW FISH HAVE EVOLVED, AS WELL AS THEIR BEHAVIOR, REPRODUCTION, AND GROWTH, THEN WRITE ABOUT IT IN SCIENTIFIC ARTICLES.

WHAT THINGS MIGHT AN ICHTHYOLOGIST DO?

- Study the natural environment of fish.
- Examine their behavior.
- Identify fish and fish species, and describe new ones.
- Monitor water quality in natural and manmade reservoirs.
- Work for the protection and safety of fish.
- Propose new research and publish findings.

LOOKING FOR NEW FISH

Ichthyologists travel to Earth's most remote places to find fish caught by local fishermen that haven't yet been listed or studied by fish experts. When they make such a discovery, they begin their research right away. Scientists have described between 20,000 and 35,000 fish species so far—more than all other vertebrates combined—and new species are discovered every year, especially in places like the Amazon River.

What's the greatest honor for an ichthyologist? To get to name a new species of fish!

FISH PROTECTION

Ichthyologists try really hard to stop fish species from dying out. They also study the fish we eat, using what they know about how these fish live to protect them from harm.

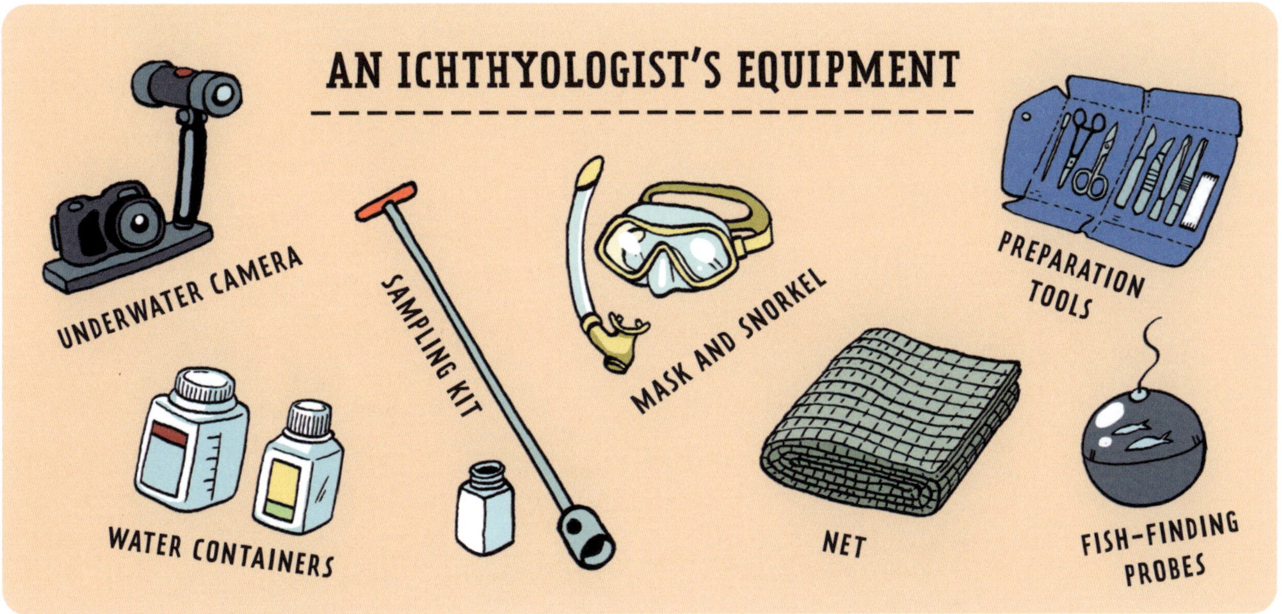

✻ BROMATOLOGIST ✻

A BROMATOLOGIST ENJOYS FOOD AND EVERYTHING ABOUT IT. THIS DOESN'T MEAN THEY ARE A BIG EATER. THEY CARE ABOUT THE QUALITY OF THE PRODUCTS ON THEIR PLATE OR IN THEIR CUP. YES—A BROMATOLOGIST IS A GENUINE FOOD SCIENTIST.

WHAT A BROMATOLOGIST MIGHT DO

- A bromatologist works on making healthy foods—like dishes low in sugar and fat—taste as good as unhealthy ones, so that in the future, we'll choose healthy options more often.

- They also come up with new flavors for yogurt and ice cream, deciding what to mix them with and how to do it. The result must be pleasing to both the eye and the taste buds. A yogurt or ice cream might taste great, but what if it's lumpy or full of ice crystals? In their testing and tasting, a bromatologist experiments with many ingredients and substances, over and over again.

• Bromatologists also think about how to store food. They search for cost-effective ways to preserve key nutrients, colors, and flavors, and explore how food can be dried or pasteurized. They analyze food composition at factories, testing it for calorie count, allergens, nutrients, sugar, fat, vitamins, and trace elements. Based on the bromatologist's analysis, the producer labels the product so customers know what nutrients they're getting when they eat it.

QUESTIONS A BROMATOLOGIST ASKS

How long does a particular food stay fresh? How should it be cooked and processed to keep its taste and important nutrients? Which preservatives can be used to keep its flavor, even when stored for months? How can we make sure it stays fresh? Is this food a healthy choice?

Everyone likes good food, but for you, is it a passion? If you enjoy checking what food is made of, what vitamins it contains, how long it stays fresh, and the best ways to keep it that way, you might be a future bromatologist.

A BROMATOLOGIST'S EQUIPMENT

* HERPETOLOGIST *

NOT ONLY DO HERPETOLOGISTS HAVE NO FEAR OF REPTILES OR AMPHIBIANS—THEY SIMPLY CAN'T IMAGINE THEIR LIVES WITHOUT THEM. HERPETOLOGISTS KNOW ALL ABOUT VENOMOUS AND NON-VENOMOUS SNAKES, LIZARDS, TORTOISES, TURTLES, FROGS, TOADS, NEWTS, CROCODILES, AND ALLIGATORS. THEY STUDY THESE COLD-BLOODED ANIMALS' BEHAVIOR, GENETICS, BODY STRUCTURE, REPRODUCTION, DISEASES, AND EVERYTHING ELSE ABOUT THEM.

FIELD AND LABORATORY

A herpetologist works both in the field and in the lab. They also do research, especially on anatomy and physiology, using museum specimens. They may care for animals directly, such as in zoos. Last but not least, they travel a lot to expand their knowledge.

Whenever others talk bad about snakes and lizards, do you get upset? Is your room filled with terrariums? You know exactly what you want to be then: a herpetologist, of course!

WHERE ARE YOU?

Mapping where reptiles and amphibians live is an important part of a herpetologist's job. They walk through the countryside looking for the animals' hiding spots (both likely and unlikely), listening to the croak of frogs, and being on the lookout for clutches of turtle eggs. They keep their eyes and ears open to understand how these creatures live in different habitats.

A HERPETOLOGIST'S EQUIPMENT

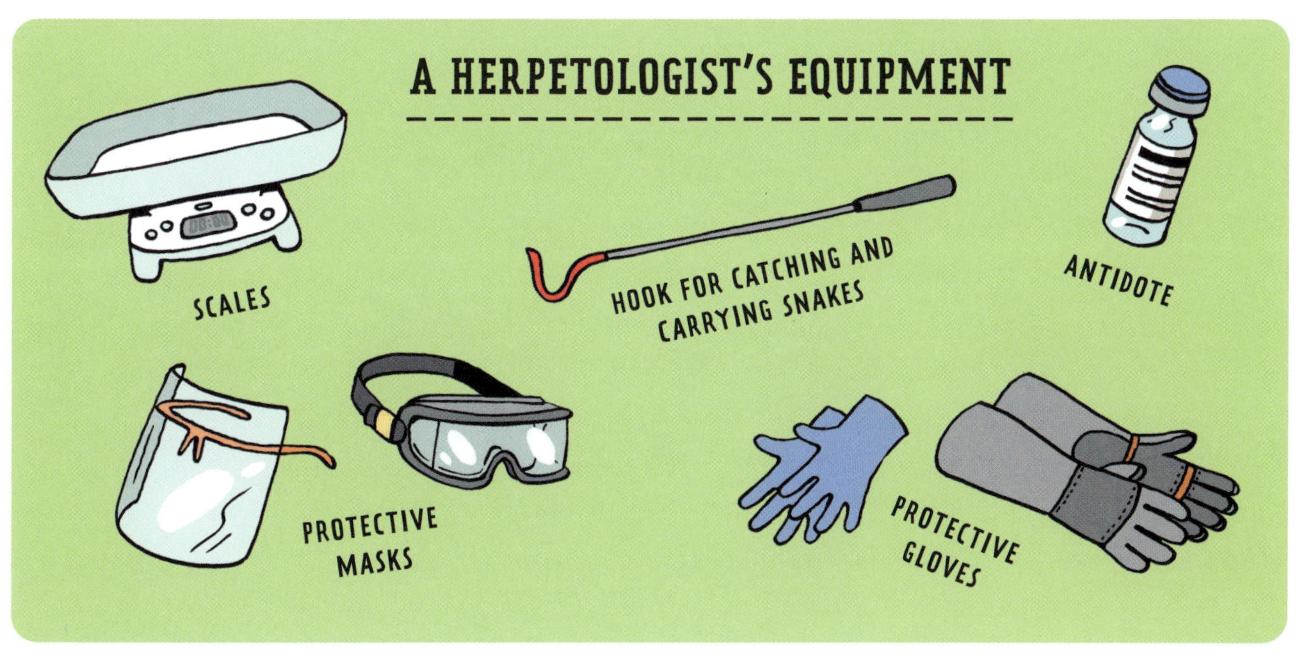

* ENTOMOLOGIST *

AN ENTOMOLOGIST IS HAPPIEST IN THE COMPANY OF BEETLES, ANTS, BUTTERFLIES, MOTHS, GRASSHOPPERS, CRICKETS, COCKROACHES, AND FLIES—IN SHORT, ALL KINDS OF INSECTS. ANYTHING WITH ANTENNAE IS SUBJECT TO THEIR ENTHUSIASTIC STUDIES AND RESEARCH.

WHAT AN ENTOMOLOGIST DOES

An entomologist travels the world in search of new species of beetles, bugs, ladybugs, and other insects. Like a detective, they track down whole groups of butterflies to study how they live. Some entomologists focus on insect pests, trying to understand their behavior so people can stop them from damaging fruit trees, ruining crops, or spreading disease.

TYPES OF ENTOMOLOGY

Entomologists are very important, busy scientists. There are millions of insects in the world, making up more than half of all living organisms. Because of this, entomology is divided into **different branches**.

COLEOPTEROLOGIST
studies beetles

MELITTOLOGIST
studies bees

HYMENOPTERIST
studies wasps

DIPTEROLOGIST
studies flies

ORTHOPTEROLOGIST
studies crickets, grasshoppers, and locusts

MYRMECOLOGIST
studies ants

LEPIDOPTEROLOGIST
studies moths and butterflies

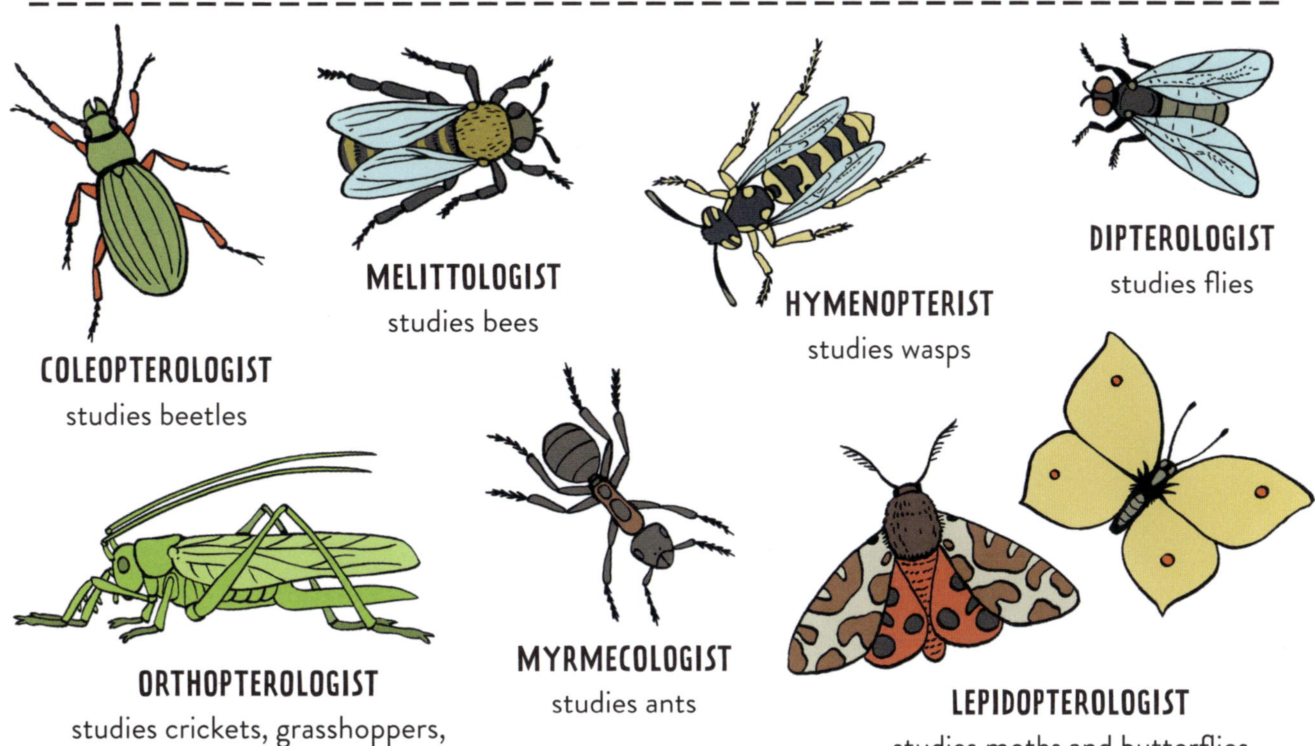

AN ENTOMOLOGIST'S EQUIPMENT

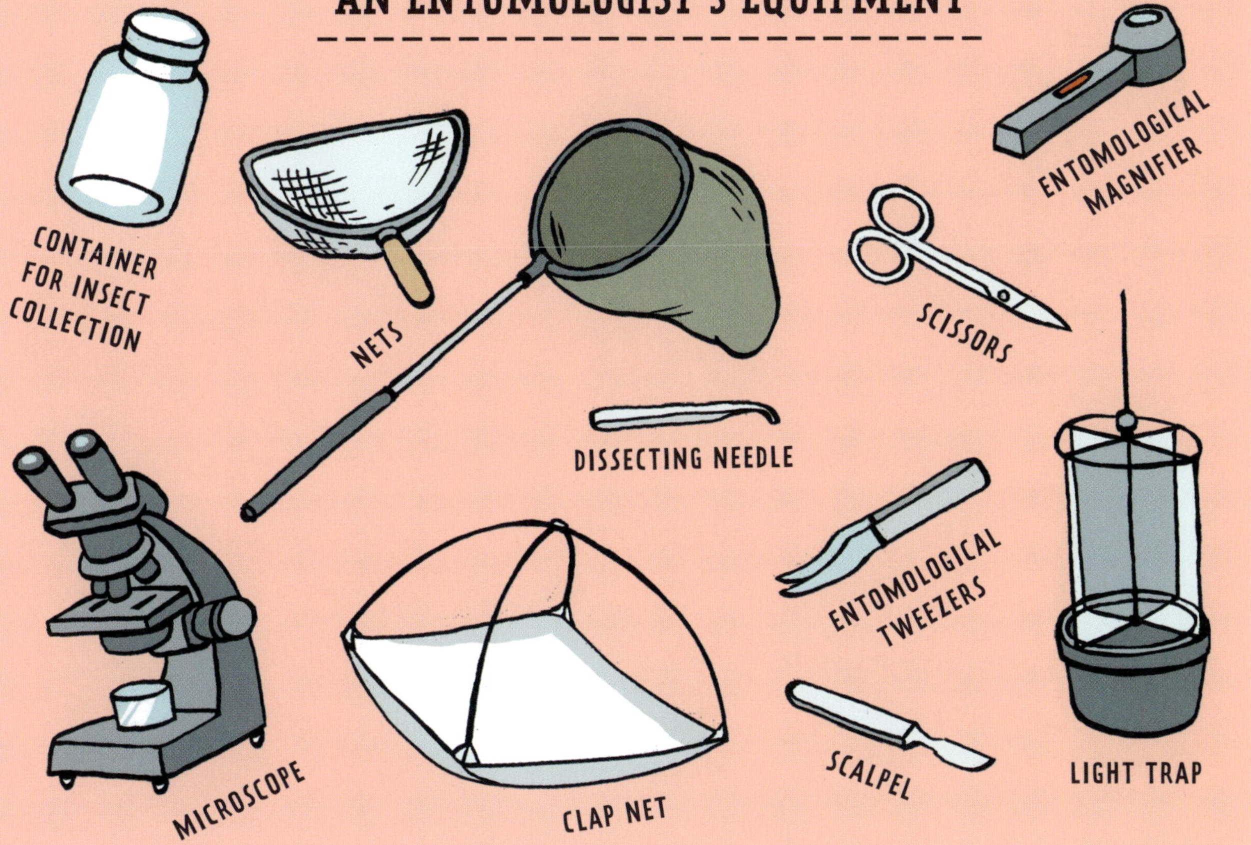

CONTAINER FOR INSECT COLLECTION
NETS
ENTOMOLOGICAL MAGNIFIER
SCISSORS
DISSECTING NEEDLE
ENTOMOLOGICAL TWEEZERS
MICROSCOPE
CLAP NET
SCALPEL
LIGHT TRAP

AN ENTOMOLOGIST'S WORK IN A NUTSHELL

An entomologist helps develop devices to protect against troublesome insects like mosquitoes.

They also develop vaccines to protect against insects that spread disease.

They study how insect species grow and change. They also examine the structure of their bodies and organs.

They observe how insects behave in different situations and conditions. They look for new species and describe them. They also study insects' structure and actions.

Some people keep aquariums, but a passionate entomologist who finds ants more interesting than fish might keep an anthill in a glass container instead.

* ORNITHOLOGIST *

AN ORNITHOLOGIST IS SO FASCINATED BY BIRDS THAT THEY SPEND THEIR CAREER STUDYING HOW BIRDS LIVE, BUILD NESTS, AND BEHAVE. SOME ORNITHOLOGISTS FOCUS ON A SPECIFIC SPECIES OR GROUP OF BIRDS, WHILE OTHERS STUDY BIRDS MORE BROADLY.

ORNITHOLOGISTS DO DIFFERENT THINGS

Ornithologists' specific duties can vary. Some study how birds live in the wild and then figure out what the observations mean. Others look at how birds are affected by changes in the environment. Some focus on genetics, how birds grow, or what diseases birds might get. Many work to protect endangered birds and help people understand why these fascinating creatures need saving.

FIELD OR OFFICE?

Don't think for a minute that an ornithologist spends all their time outdoors, watching birds through binoculars or recording bird calls. Most of their day is spent on a computer, studying what they've observed or analyzing test results.

WHAT AN ORNITHOLOGIST DOES IN THE FIELD

In the field, an ornithologist might count birds and study their nesting habits—how they build nests, raise their chicks, and find food. These scientists also watch courtship behaviors and tag birds to estimate population sizes and to determine whether a species is at risk. The data are later studied in the lab.

AN ORNITHOLOGIST'S EQUIPMENT

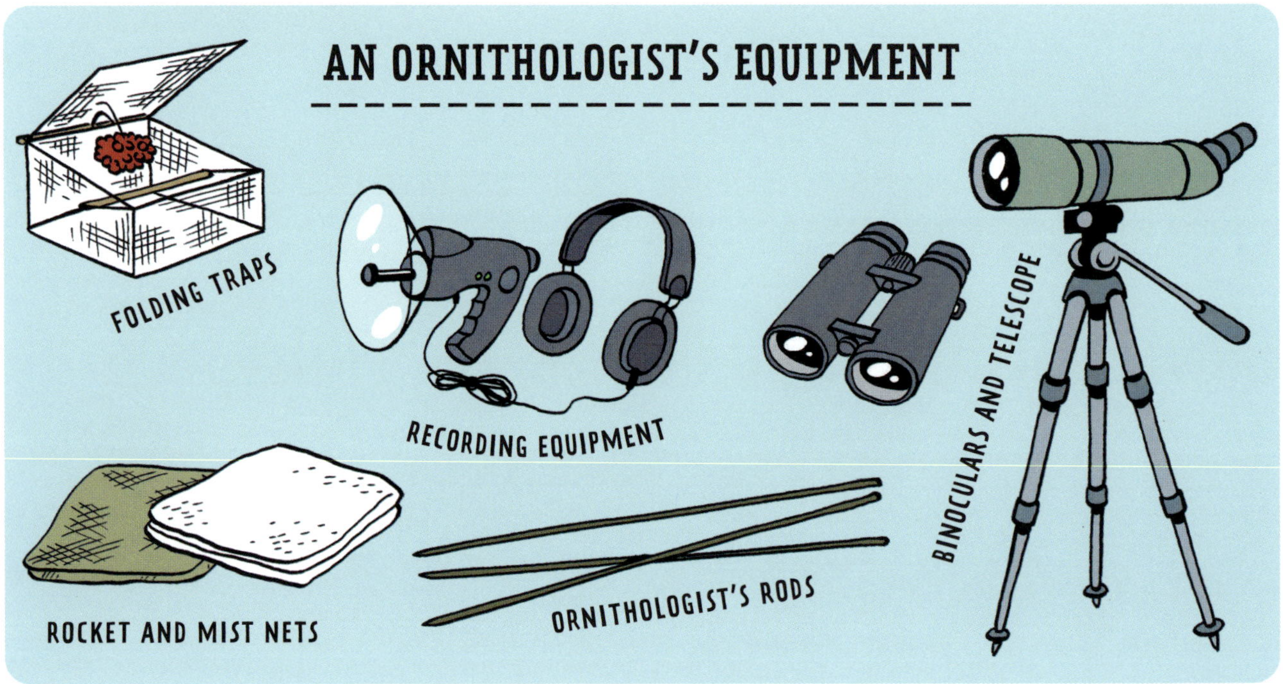

AN ORNITHOLOGIST'S WORK IN A NUTSHELL

- In the field, they study where different species live, and migrate, and how quickly birds reproduce.
- They track bird populations and the health of different species.

- They follow birds' movements and gather information on overall bird numbers.
- They work on projects to protect and care for birds.
- They also write reports and scientific studies.

AN ORNITHOLOGIST IN A LABORATORY

In a lab, an ornithologist can study feathers to learn about bird genetics. They might also observe birds that were injured or raised in captivity to better understand behavior, diet, or communication. After completing their research, they write about their findings and share them in science magazines and other publications.

Can you identify a bird by its song? If you see a bird you don't recognize, do you look it up? If you're curious about birds, maybe becoming an ornithologist is your dream!

* PARASITOLOGIST *

You think lice, ticks, and microscopic parasites are fascinating. You might not want them on or in your body, but you love learning about their traits. The world needs more parasitologists, so why not become one?

A PARASITOLOGIST ISN'T AFRAID TO STUDY ANY PARASITE, EXAMINING HOW THEY INTERACT WITH THEIR HOST AND THE DAMAGE THEY MAY CAUSE. THESE SCIENTISTS HAVE NO FEAR OF FLEAS, LICE, TICKS, OR CREATURES TOO SMALL TO SEE.

UNWANTED RELATIONS

In most cases, a person, plant, or animal—the host—doesn't want a parasite and tries to make it as unwelcome and uncomfortable as possible. But parasites have skills! They cling on tightly, hide, and do everything they can to adapt to the host's defenses. This ongoing battle for survival is so fascinating to the parasitologist that they study it day and night.

HOW TO DEAL WITH PARASITES

Some parasitologists study parasites that affect people. They learn how parasites cause diseases like malaria and typhus. Their main goal is to create vaccines to protect us from diseases caused by things like ticks and mosquitoes.

SEARCHING FOR PARASITES

Another group of parasitologists studies parasites that live on animals or plants. This is really important because people eat these animals or plants, or, in the case of pets, live with them.

Along with working in labs to create vaccines, these parasitologists also travel the world to learn more about known parasites and find new ones. It's important to keep all parasites under control!

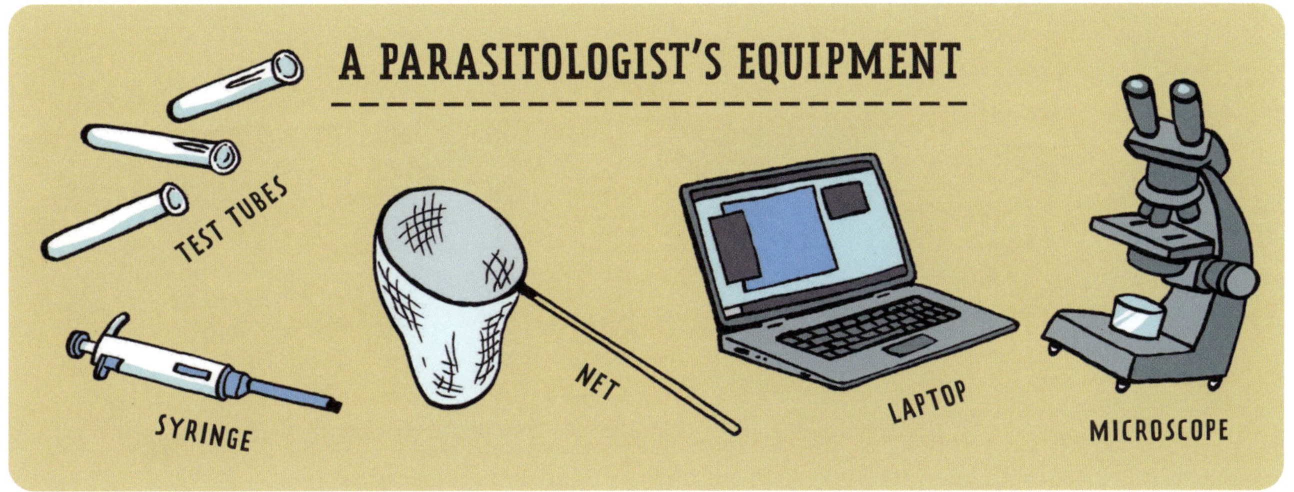

* DENDROLOGIST *

A DENDROLOGIST IS A SCIENTIST WHO STUDIES TREES, SHRUBS, AND ALL OTHER WOODY PLANTS THAT GROW OR HAVE EVER GROWN ON EARTH. ASK THEM ANYTHING ABOUT LEAVES, NEEDLES, OR ANYTHING ELSE RELATED TO TREES, AND THEY WILL KNOW THE ANSWER.

WHAT A DENDROLOGIST DOES

First and foremost, dendrologists can recognize different species and subspecies of trees, shrubs, and other woody plants, spotting even the smallest differences between them. They use this knowledge to create guides that help others understand the world of plants. At the same time, they carefully describe newly discovered species.

CONES, POLLEN, BARK

Dendrologists study not just the overall characteristics of trees and woody plants, but also their leaves, needles, cones, fruit, flowers, bark, and complex root systems. They work to understand the purpose of each part and also explore how these plants reproduce, including studying pollen.

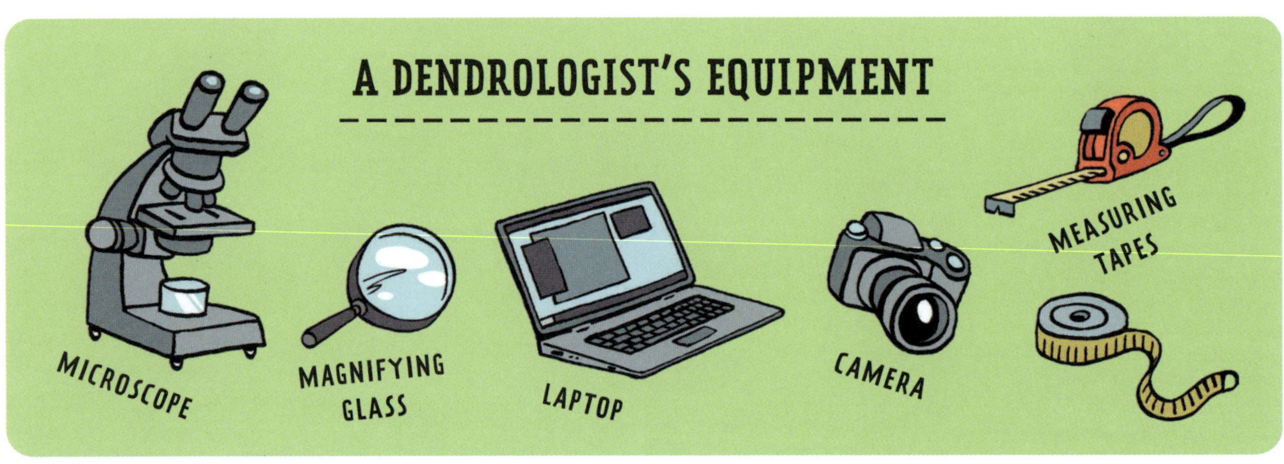

* GLACIOLOGIST *

A GLACIOLOGIST LOVES COLD WINTERS. IN FACT, THEY ARE SO FASCINATED BY ICE AND SNOW THAT THEY STUDY THEM EVERY DAY, PAYING CLOSE ATTENTION TO EVERY DETAIL. NO ONE UNDERSTANDS ICE AND SNOW BETTER THAN A GLACIOLOGIST.

GLACIER RESEARCH

A glaciologist studies large bodies of ice and snow called glaciers. These scientists look at how glaciers move and grow, and how they change because of the climate crisis. Glaciologists are also interested in snow, ice caps on mountains, and areas where the ground stays frozen all the time (called permafrost).

RETURN JOURNEYS

There are glaciers on every continent except Australia, so a glaciologist travels a lot. They spend time at special research stations, watching the glaciers and the environment around them. To help with their studies, they set up special outdoor instruments and place markers on glaciers to track how they move.

CHANGES ARE COMING

A glaciologist collects samples of snow and ice. By examining ice from cracks in glaciers, they can learn about past climate conditions and how much snow has fallen each year.

THE FUTURE OF THE PLANET

A glaciologist shares their research findings with other scientists and the public at conferences. Everyone should care about the future of our planet. Thanks to their work, glaciologists can predict how Earth will change due to the climate crisis.

Are snow and ice more than just winter fun to you? Are you fascinated by the many types of snow and the uniqueness of each snowflake? Does ice capture your attention with its beauty? If you answered yes, then a career as a glaciologist could be in your future!

ON EARTH AS IT IS IN HEAVEN

A glaciologist's knowledge goes beyond just snow and ice on Earth. Ice and snow are also found on other planets in our solar system. By studying them, scientists discover fascinating details about these distant worlds.

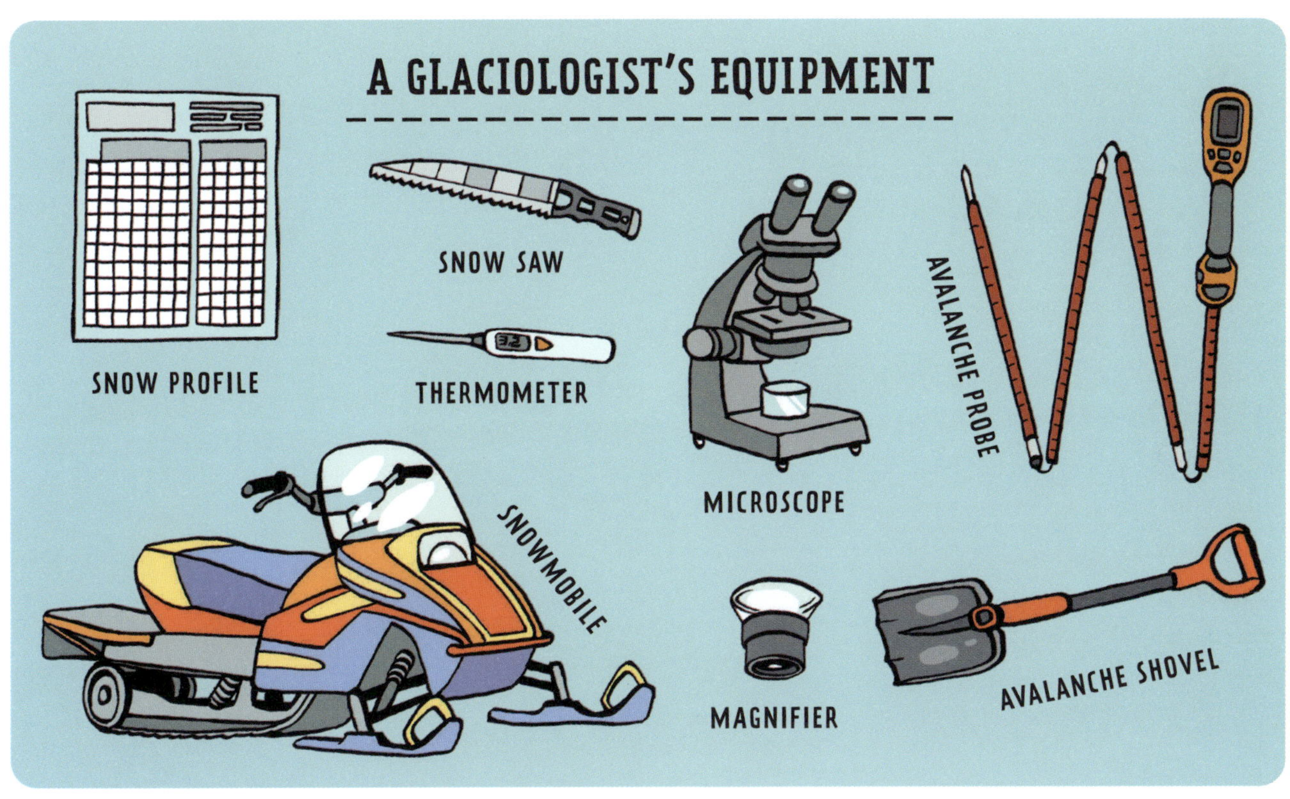

* MUSICOLOGIST *

What was the popular music of prehistory? What did medieval kings listen to? What instruments did people used to play? Do animals like music? If you ask yourself such questions, perhaps musicology is the science for you!

MUSICOLOGISTS STUDY MUSIC, EXPLORE ITS HISTORY, AND UNDERSTAND HOW IT WORKS. THEY KNOW PRACTICALLY EVERYTHING THERE IS TO KNOW ABOUT MUSIC—EVEN WHEN IT'S 1,000 YEARS OLD!

HOORAY FOR TRAVEL

Some musicologists travel a lot for their work. Their curiosity about the music of different cultures takes them all over the world. They record traditional songs and melodies, and learn about the unique instruments used by different nations.

HISTORY OF MUSIC

What music was played during the Gothic, Renaissance, and Baroque periods? And what instruments were used? This is the kind of question a musicologist might study. They explore the features of music from these eras, the sounds of the instruments used, and how these sounds are different from modern instruments. A musicologist might also research how people reacted to the music in those days—did they enjoy it, or did they throw rotten eggs at the musicians?

Hmm. I imagine that many eggs were wasted on medieval musicians. . . .

PSYCHOLOGY OF MUSIC

Musicologists also study how music affects the mind. For example, in advertisements, the right music can make people want to buy a product—even in large quantities!

MUSIC AND ANIMALS

Who can say if music exists in the animal kingdom? Some musicologists try to answer this question. They test how animals react to different types of music and even create music for specific animal species.

For example, musicologists have found that dogs are calmed by classical music, cows produce more milk when listening to relaxing tunes, and cats and monkeys seem totally uninterested in human music. Interestingly, a bird's brain reacts to music in a similar way to a human's!

COMPOSITION STUDY

Let's say a famous composer didn't live long enough to finish their last works. What will happen to these incomplete pieces? Thankfully, musicologists are here to help! One of their jobs is to complete these unfinished compositions.

MUSIC AND LIFE

A carefully selected melody can positively affect a baby growing in the womb and help soothe premature babies. Listening to music regularly can even strengthen an adult's immune system. Who discovered all this? Why, musicologists, of course!

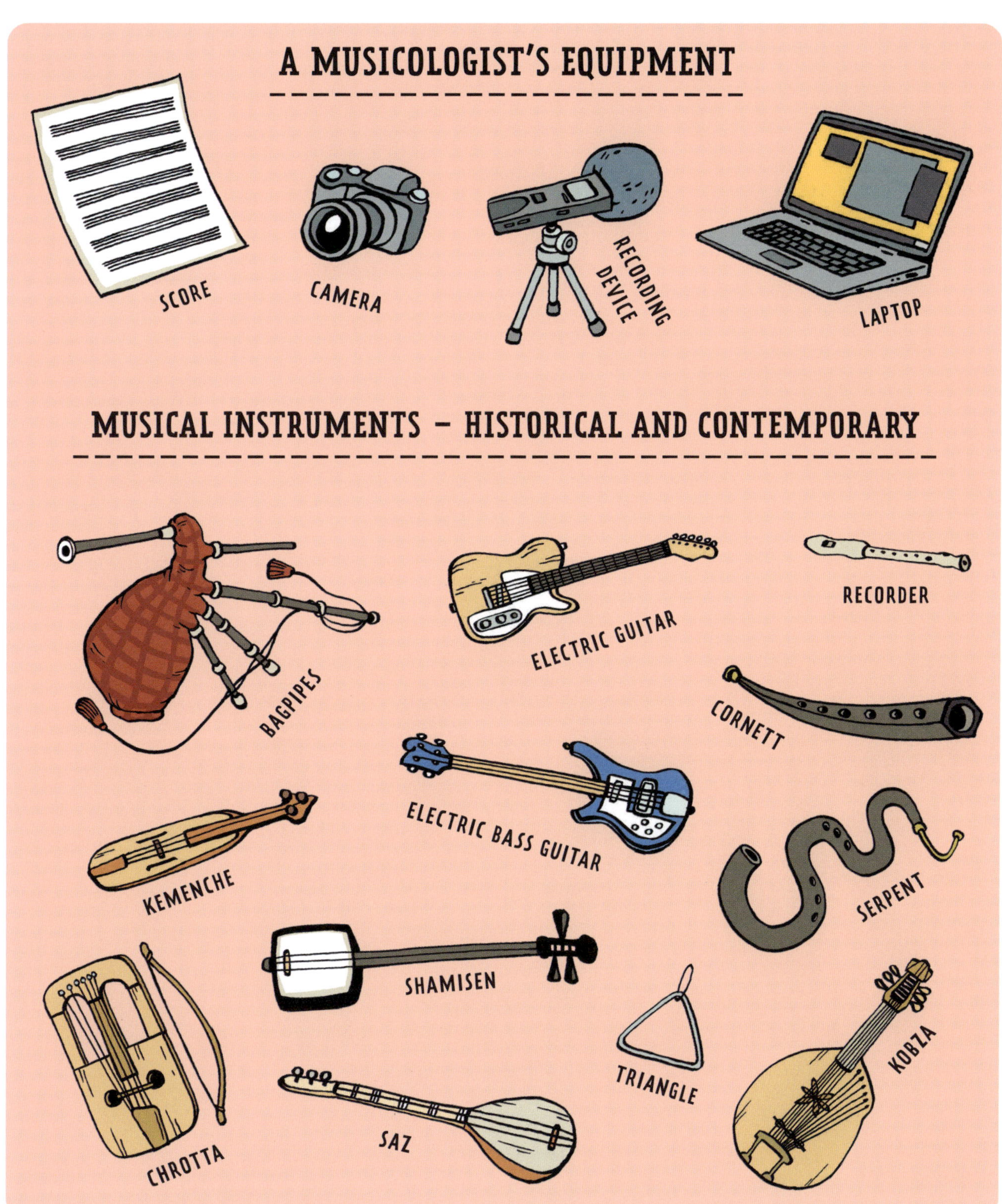

TYPES OF MUSICOLOGY

Musicology is a diverse science that covers a lot of fields, including:
ETHNOMUSICOLOGY – deals with musical traditions.
ZOOMUSICOLOGY – seeks to discover if and how music exists among animals.
ORGANOLOGY – studies the structures, properties, and development of musical instruments.
And there are a ton more!

* MYCOLOGIST *

A MYCOLOGIST IS A PASSIONATE COLLECTOR OF MUSHROOMS WHO STUDIES MOLDS AND YEASTS, WHICH ARE ALSO TYPES OF FUNGI. THEY MAY NOT UNDERSTAND EVERYTHING ABOUT THE HUGE WORLD OF FUNGI RIGHT AWAY, BUT THEY'RE EXCELLENT AT SOLVING MYSTERIES.

WHERE A MYCOLOGIST IS AT HOME

Some mycologists go on trips to find new mushrooms and molds. Others grow their own mushrooms, yeasts, and molds to see how they can be useful to people—like for making energy from plants, called biofuels, which can be used instead of oil or gas.

Do you find fungi the most interesting organisms in the world? Do you know your fungi encyclopedia inside and out and are excited to share what you've learned? Well then, you're a born mycologist!

MYCOLOGISTS IN FIELDS AND ORCHARDS

Mycologists also work in fields with farm crops and orchards, where plants and trees might get attacked by harmful mold. And who knows about this mold? Mycologists, of course! They're the ones who prevent or treat diseases that could harm the crops.

INTEREST IN LICHENS

Mycologists are also interested in lichens, which are formed when fungi work together with algae or cyanobacteria. A mycologist who specializes in lichens is called a lichenologist.

How are mycology and pharmaceutical products related? Some medicines have a fungal component.

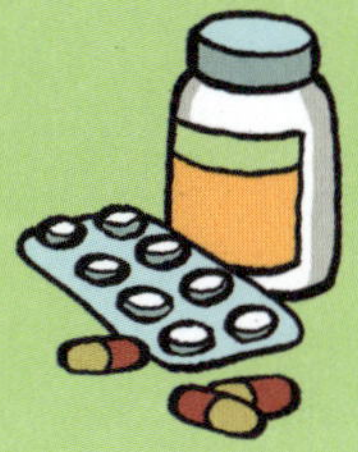

Did you know that there is such a thing as a specialist fungus farm?

RESEARCHING DISEASE

Don't think that all mycologists are just out in the woods collecting mushrooms. Some work in hospitals, where they focus on fungi that cause diseases in humans. These mycologists study harmful fungi to understand and treat infections.

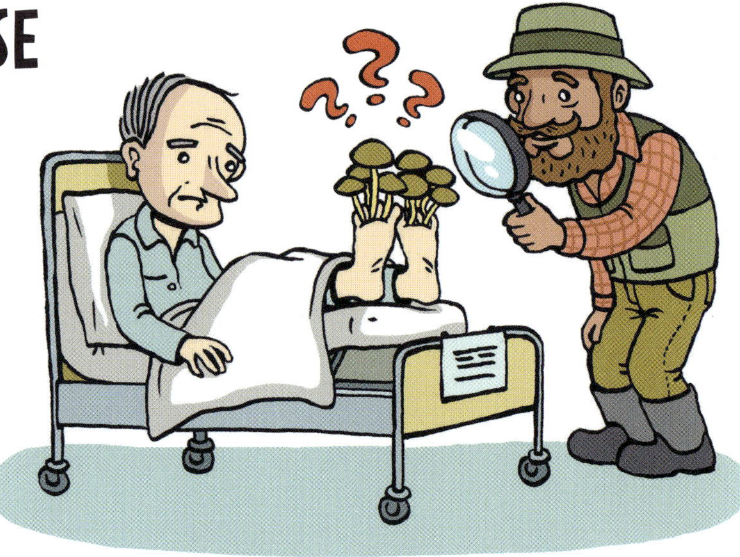

Why isn't it rising and foaming? I must have made a basic scientific error. . . .

WHY ISN'T IT RISING?

Mycologists are a big help to brewers and bakers because they love yeast! Yeasts are the most common and useful fungi in the world. Without them, we wouldn't have beer or bread. Mycologists work to discover new types of yeast and come up with new recipes for making these foods.

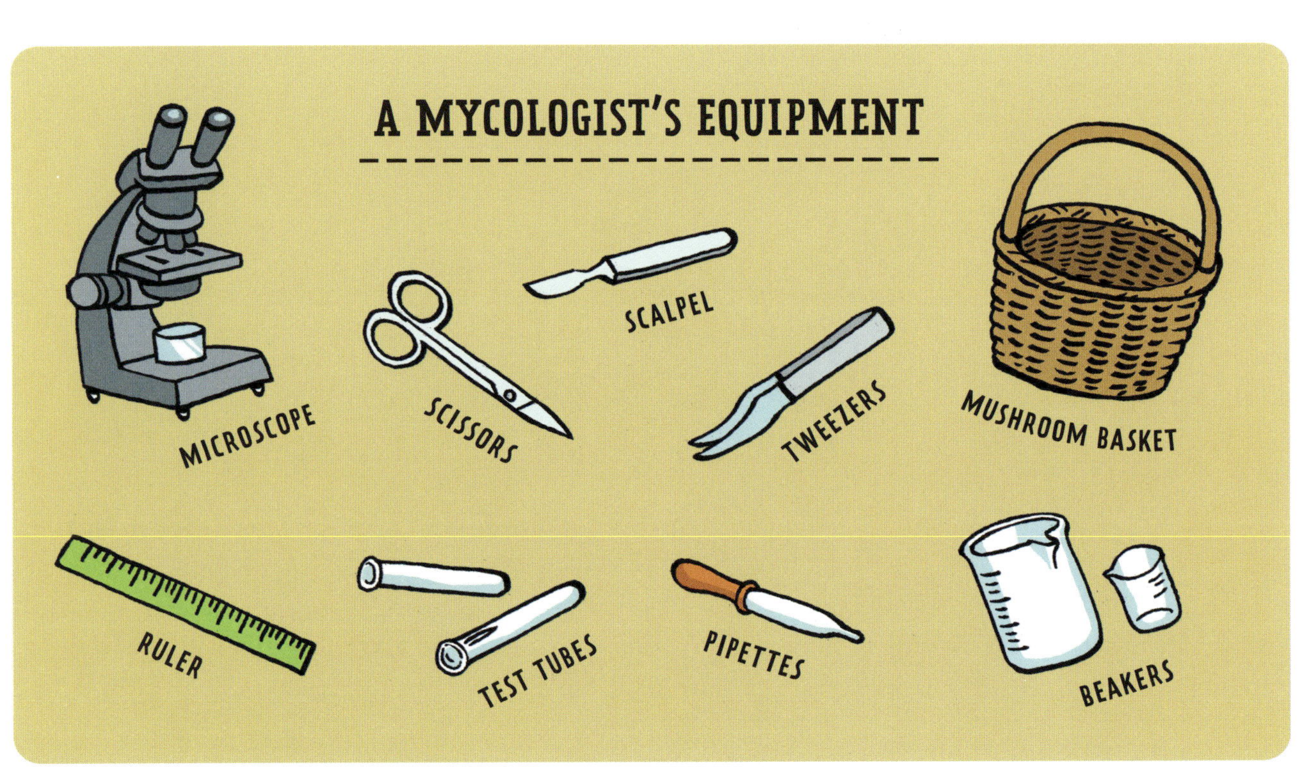

* GEOLOGIST *

A GEOLOGIST LOVES ROCKS, STONES, AND MINERALS, AND TRAVELS TO THE MOST REMOTE PLACES TO STUDY THEM. GEOLOGISTS ARE ALSO INTERESTED IN VOLCANOES, INCLUDING THEIR SOIL, LAYERS, AND THE RESOURCES INSIDE THEM LIKE OIL, WATER, AND ICE. BY EXPLORING EARTH IN DETAIL, THE SCIENTISTS TRY TO UNDERSTAND HOW OUR PLANET HAS CHANGED OVER TIME AND WHAT'S HAPPENING NOW TO HELP US BETTER UNDERSTAND THE FUTURE. GEOLOGISTS ALSO STUDY ROCKS FROM THE MOON AND OTHER PLANETS.

GEOLOGIC MAP

An important part of a geologist's work is creating geologic maps, which show the types of rocks found in a certain area, along with their age and condition.

RED INDICATES GRANITE. DARK GREEN INDICATES IGNEOUS ROCK.

GEOLOGICAL ANALYSES

MICROSCOPIC ANALYSIS

is the examination of rocks, minerals, and fossils in the tiniest detail ... under a microscope, of course.

GEOCHEMICAL ANALYSIS

is research into the composition of geological samples. It can determine metal content and the quality of oil in a given well.

GEOMECHANICAL ANALYSIS

is testing and determining the strength of a newly found rock.

FIELD WORK IS THE BEST!

Most of a geologist's work is done in the field. Since this can be dangerous, they wear a high-visibility vest and protective helmet to stay safe from falling rocks.

LAB WORK

Don't think that geologists spend all their time outdoors. They also work in a laboratory, where they examine, analyze, and study their samples to learn more about them.

Do you come back from every walk with pockets full of stones, eager to examine them? Afterward, do you try to learn their names and discover what they look like inside? Are you curious about rock formations? It sounds like you're on your way to becoming a geologist.

3D MODELING

Clever geologists also use computers. They create special programs to model things like oil fields, mineral deposits, and more. These models help them with their research.

BUILDING A HOUSE? CALL A GEOLOGIST

If you plan to build a house, don't forget to get a geologist's survey. A geologist will check if the soil is good for building and help tell you how to build your house so it stays safe, even if the ground beneath isn't as strong as you think!

FIELDS OF GEOLOGY

MARINE GEOLOGY – study of the seabed, beaches, and estuaries.
PETROLEUM GEOLOGY – study of the search for oil deposits and exploration of oil.
PLANETARY GEOLOGY – study of the geology of planets, their moons, comets, asteroids, and meteorites.
HYDROGEOLOGY – study of the properties of natural groundwater.

A GEOLOGIST'S EQUIPMENT

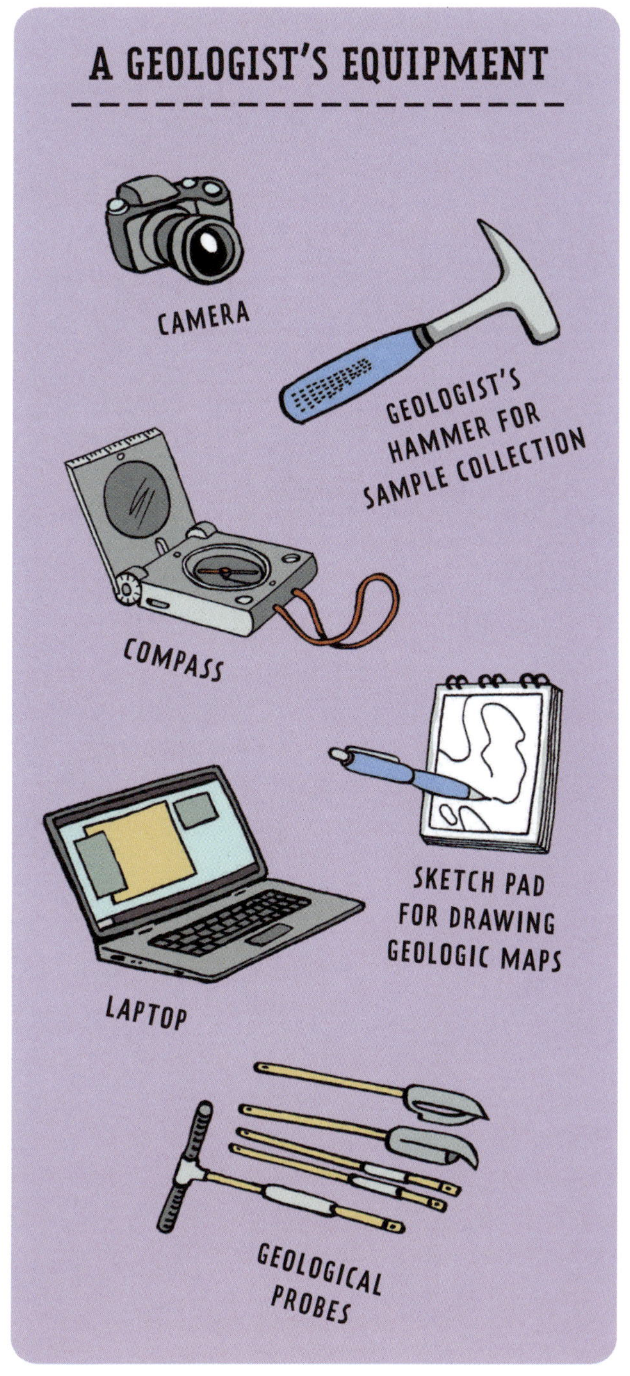

* PEDOLOGIST *

A PEDOLOGIST CAN'T GET ENOUGH SOIL, SAND, OR CLAY. THEY DON'T MIND GETTING THEIR HANDS DIRTY—IN FACT, THEY LOVE IT! THEY KNOW A LOT ABOUT DIFFERENT TYPES OF SOIL AND EVEN ENJOY ITS SMELL!

HANDS IN THE SOIL

A pedologist studies different types of soil, looks at how they formed, and describes their characteristics. Some soils let water pass through easily and have lots of nutrients, making them more fertile. Others don't let water through and are infertile. A pedologist can spot these differences and give helpful advice to gardeners and farmers.

THE COLOR OF SOIL

Pedologists work outside, collecting samples of different types of soil. Once they have enough, they bring the samples back to the lab, and check things like color, texture, minerals, moisture, and temperature. There's a lot to do!

You might think that soil is just black or brown, but it can actually be a wide range of colors, like blue, red, and pink. The color of the soil helps pedologists understand how it formed and how it holds water.

Soil may seem plain, but if you look closely, you'll notice that one type might be dark and another light and powdery. To really understand the ground beneath your feet, you need to study it. Maybe you'd like to become a pedologist!

SOLVING PROBLEMS

Being a pedologist means working on important problems. They help solve issues like soil loss or plants getting sick because of bad soil. Plants give us food, and soil is super important for the environment. It affects water, plants, and animals. Without soil, we couldn't live!

There's nothing complicated about it. For instance, a blue soil has been wet for many years and the iron has been leached out of it.

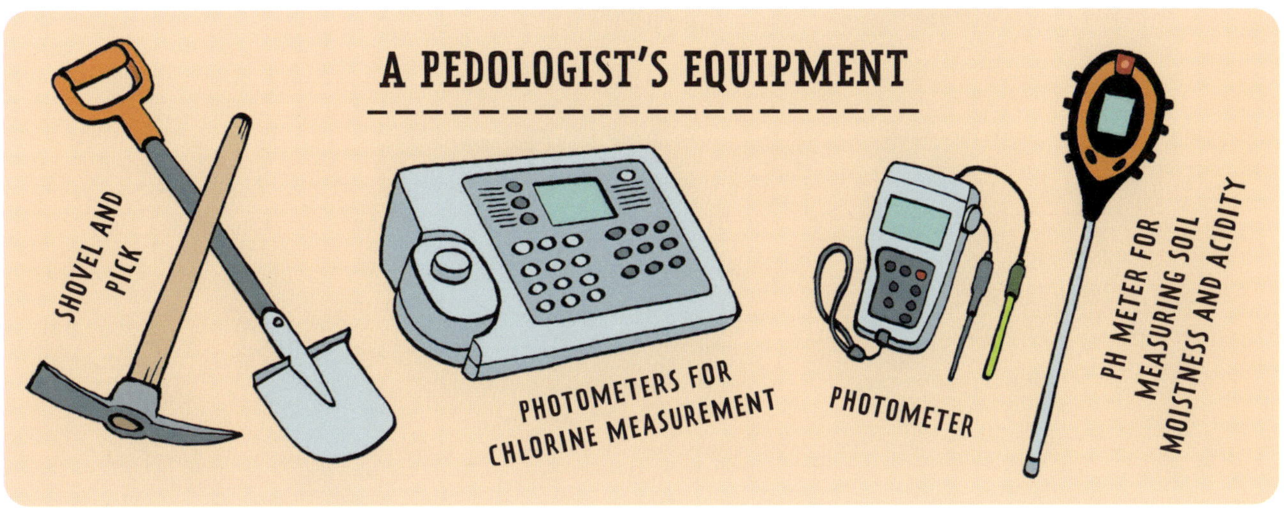

* HYDROLOGIST *

A HYDROLOGIST HAS CHOSEN TO SPEND THEIR LIFE STUDYING WATER. THEY LOOK AT WATER IN ALL ITS FORMS: AS STEAM, LIQUID, AND ICE. THEY STUDY HOW WATER MOVES, THE WATER CYCLE, AND THE PROPERTIES OF WATER ON THE SURFACE AND UNDERGROUND.

If you could, you'd grow fins and live in the water. Whether it's salty or fresh, water is everything to you. Water is life! How about becoming a hydrologist?

WHAT A HYDROLOGIST DOES

Hydrologists collect samples from rivers, lakes, and underground sources to see what's in the water. They study how rainfall affects rivers and look for any signs that the water is polluted. They also find ways to fix problems with water quality.

The river flow is at record levels! This is almost unheard of!

I'm taking water samples to closely study in the lab.

I see that the water level keeps falling. This dreadful drought!

Where do the distributaries lead? I hope I've got this right. . . .

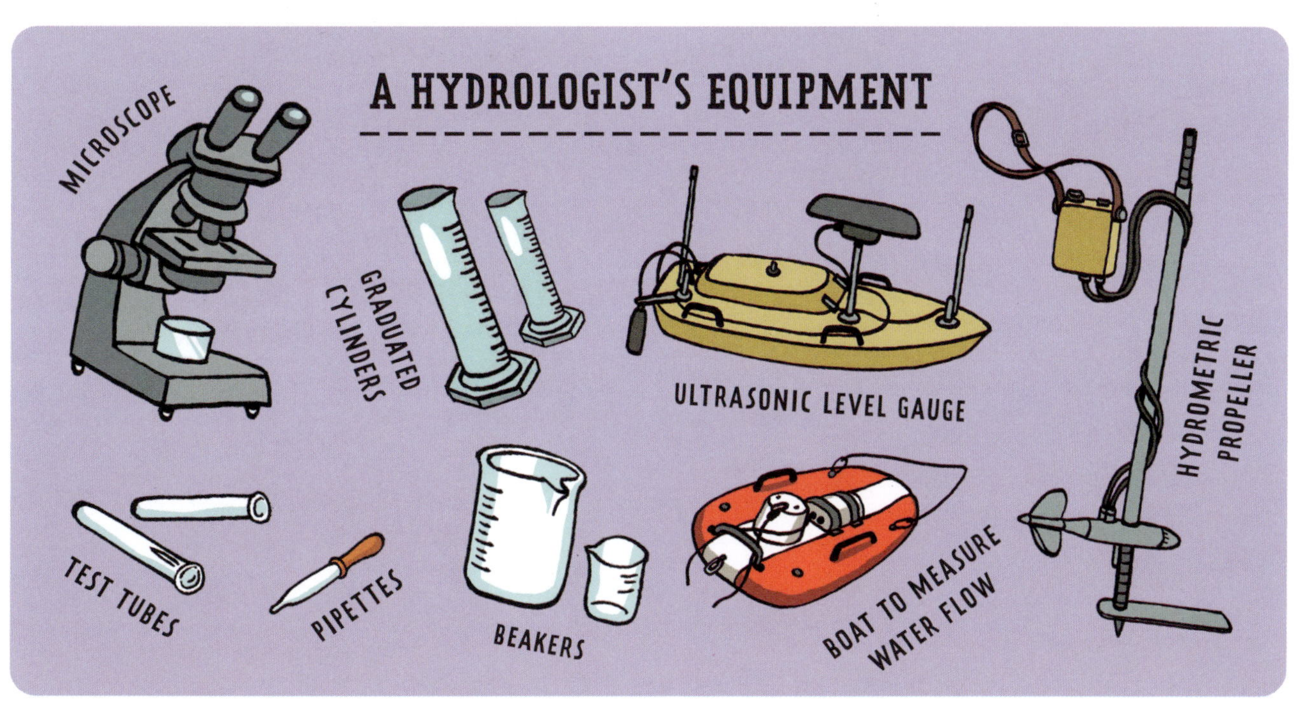

* ANTHROPOLOGIST *

AN ANTHROPOLOGIST IS FASCINATED BY HUMANKIND AND HUMAN SOCIETIES AND CIVILIZATIONS. THEY ARE SUPER-CURIOUS ABOUT PEOPLE AND ARE ALWAYS LOOKING FOR ANSWERS, EITHER ON THEIR COMPUTER OR IN THE FIELD. WHEN STUDYING THE DISTANT PAST, THEY WORK CLOSELY WITH ARCHAEOLOGISTS. LIKE AN ARCHAEOLOGIST, AN ANTHROPOLOGIST LOOKS FOR ARTIFACTS.

Do you love books and films about indigenous people who live in the rainforest? Are you interested in rituals and the human tendency to socialize in different groups? If so, you're well on your way to becoming an anthropologist.

SOME ANTHROPOLOGIST QUESTIONS

How has human civilization grown? How have natural disasters affected human evolution? What is the role of language among humans? What does a pet mean to a group of pet owners? Why isn't bullfighting seen as animal cruelty by its fans? What makes humans different from other species?

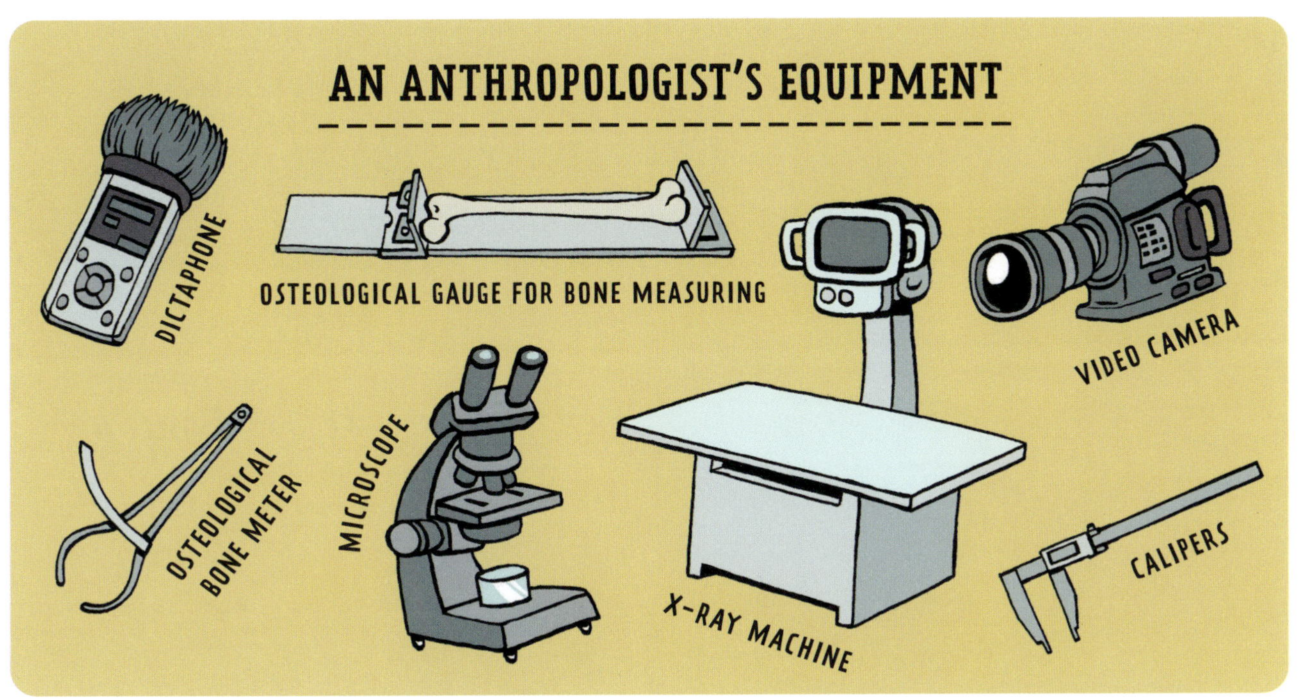

WHAT IT TAKES TO BE AN ANTHROPOLOGIST

We can sort anthropologists into different groups based on what they study. A physical anthropologist looks at how humans have evolved over time. They study diseases and problems that old rulers, monarchs, and famous people had, and even recreate the faces of our ancient ancestors by looking at their skulls. A linguistic anthropologist focuses on how people talk to each other and how language changes over time.

A sociocultural anthropologist studies the customs and behaviors of different groups of people. Some of them go to very remote places in the world to live with indigenous people and learn about their ways of life, traditions, and rituals. Other anthropologists work with specific groups of people to understand how these groups are organized and how they came to be. In short, these scientists want to learn everything about humans. As you can imagine, an anthropologist is rarely alone!

* UFOLOGIST *

A UFOLOGIST IS INTERESTED IN THE MYSTERIES OF OUTER SPACE. THEY WISH TO PROVE THE EXISTENCE OF EXTRATERRESTRIAL CIVILIZATIONS AND REVEAL THAT CERTAIN UNIDENTIFIED FLYING OBJECTS—UFO'S—ARE REAL.

IS IT THEM?

Not all UFO's are flying saucers with aliens inside, you know. The unidentified object might be an airplane, a bird, or something completely different. A ufologist works hard to figure out what was really seen in the sky by investigating and explaining what it could have been.

CROP CIRCLES

Ufologists are also curious about crop circles, which some people believe are messages from alien civilizations. However, most of the time, a mysterious circle turns out to be the work of pranksters who trample the crops at night.

DID YOU SEE THAT?

Ufologists are eager to prove that extraterrestrial civilizations exist. So, when someone says they saw aliens, a ufologist will ask them and any possible witnesses lots of questions, just like a detective. They need strong proof to believe the story.

ACADEMIA

Don't think a ufologist is just daydreaming about aliens. While doing their research, they work with respected scientists like psychologists, psychiatrists, and astronomers. They even team up with the army. They try to keep their research fair and based on facts.

A UFOLOGIST'S EQUIPMENT

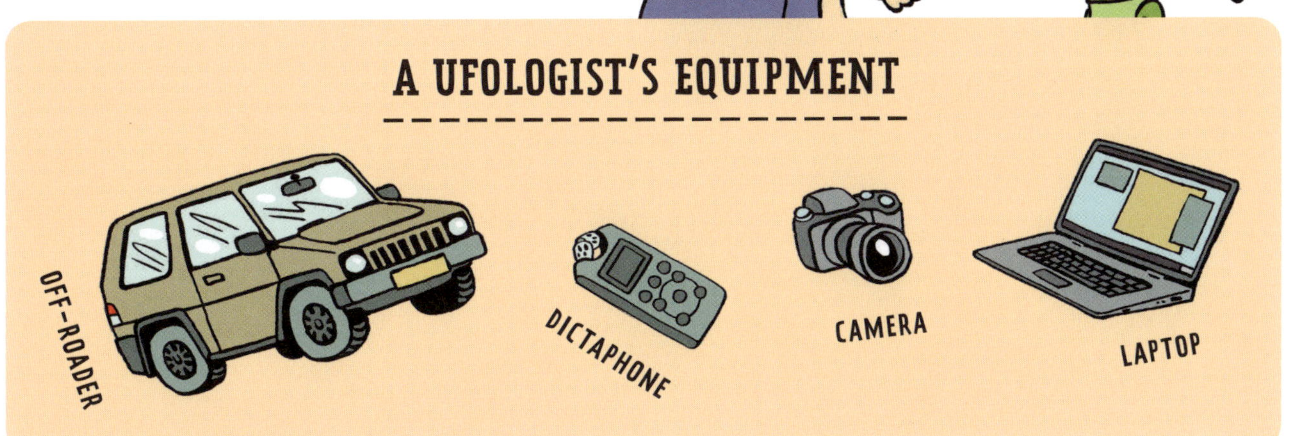

HAVE YOU READ THIS BOOK WITH CARE AND ATTENTION?

1.

A HYDROLOGIST STUDIES WATER. WHICH OF THESE ACTIVITIES DO THEY *NOT* PERFORM?

A) They measure water flow and collect and analyze samples.

B) They measure water levels.

C) They add salt to seawater.

2.

WHAT DO YOU CALL FISH SCIENTIST?

A) A fisherman

B) A water goblin

C) An ichthyologist

3.

WHICH OF THE FOLLOWING ANIMALS ARE PARASITES?

A) A *Tyrannosaurus rex*

B) A tick

C) A cuckoo bird

4.

WHICH SCIENTIST STUDIES MOSSES AND SIMILAR PLANTS?

A) A bryologist

B) A mossologist

C) A dendrologist

5.

WHERE DOES A GLACIOLOGIST TRAVEL FOR WORK?

A) To the desert—they study how sand reacts to sunlight.

B) To regions covered in snow and ice, to study glaciers.

C) To rainforests—their research aims to put carnivorous plants on a vegetarian diet.

IF SO, THIS QUIZ WILL BE CHILD'S PLAY FOR YOU.

WHICH OF THESE MUSICAL INSTRUMENTS ARE PICTURED IN THE MUSICOLOGIST CHAPTER?

A) Bagpipes, triangle, recorder

B) Recorder, electric guitar, piano

C) Shamisen, saxophone, drum

WHO IS INTERESTED IN THE MYSTERIES OF SPACE?

A) A mysteriologist

B) An astrologist

C) A ufologist

WHAT CAN AN ARCHAEOLOGIST NOT DO WITHOUT?

A) Superglue

B) A decent shovel

C) A snack

WHICH REPTILE IS PICTURED IN THE HERPETOLOGIST CHAPTER?

A) A cobra

B) A sea turtle

C) A chameleon

IF YOU DON'T KNOW ANY OF THE ANSWERS, HERE THEY ARE:

1C, 2C, 3B, 4A, 5B, 6A, 7C, 8B, 9C

I want to be a

SCIENTIST

Written by **Štěpánka Sekaninová**
Illustrated by **Honza Smolík**

5. května 1746/22, Prague 4, Czech Republic
Author: Štěpánka Sekaninová
Illustrator: © Honza Smolík, 2024
Editor: Bohdana Jarošová
Translator: Andrew Oakland
Proofreader: Susan Marston
Graphics and typesetting: Martin Urbánek and Roman Havlice

Printed in China by Leo Paper Products Co., Ltd.

www.albatrosbooks.com

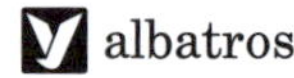